"Michael Schick has distilled weighty wisdom into practical, accessible nuggets of gold in this short book. It will help anyone who wants to live intentionally, with purpose and significance, in the workplace arenas of this frazzled world!"

ELLEN VAUGHN
New York Times **bestselling author of** *Come, Sit, Stay*

"I love the definition of 'Bible'—'Basic Instruction Before Leaving Earth'! But while we're fighting the daily battle on Planet Earth, who's responsible for my life? God or me? *God's Job, Our Job* helps clarify these two roles, and shows how both God and man working together can help people find abundant life, even in the midst of struggles."

MARABEL MORGAN
Bestselling author of *The Total Woman* **and** *Total Joy*

"If you want a book about your purpose on this planet that is not only concise, but profound and practical, then get *God's Job, Our Job*. Mike Schick brilliantly puts God's purposes for all of us in a compact thirty-one-day format. He also asks pointed questions that will help you align your job with God's job. Life changing!"

FRANK TUREK
Coauthor of *I Don't Have Enough Faith to Be an Atheist*

"*God's Job, Our Job* is a helpful exploration of the Christian's declaration of dependence on Christ. It highlights the tasks he's given us to do in loving response to his ultimate work for us on the cross. The simplicity and clarity are excellent."

JOANNE KEMP
Wife of the late Honorable Jack Kemp

"Michael Schick has written a devotional with a difference. It is a thirty-one-day exploration of the character of God (in action) and your response to God's call on your life. The theology is sound, the writing crisp and clear, and the applications of great benefit. I highly recommend taking this journey."

ART LINDSLEY
Senior Fellow, C. S. Lewis Institute
and author of *C. S. Lewis's Case for Christ*

"*God's Job, Our Job* is a wonderful devotional that simply defines and reminds us of who God is and what he has accomplished for us. I truly pray for wisdom to live out the job I'm reminded to live in this special book."

STEVEN V. TAYLOR
Nine-time Dove Award–winning producer,
arranger and songwriter

"Elegant and pithy, *God's Job, Our Job* shows us how much more effective we are if we allow God to do His work without our getting in the way, and if we figure out what our role as His creatures should be."

DAVID AIKMAN
Professor of history, Patrick Henry College,
and author of *One Nation Without God*

"I have known Michael almost thirty years, and he is for real—the kind of person worth listening to. Michael has acquired a real insight into what matters and what doesn't matter. I believe you will be blessed by this little book."

JERRY LEACHMAN
Former Chaplain, Washington Redskins

"I think *God's Job, Our Job* is a terrific format—very refreshing in its brevity and straightforwardness. It's easy to use individually or in a group setting."

DAVID R. BOCK
Former World Bank executive
and investment banker

2/1/16

GOD'S JOB

Knowing the Difference Makes All the Difference

OUR JOB

To My Good Friend, Lewis —

May This Little Book Be
A Big Encouragement To
You.

God's Best!

GOD'S JOB

Knowing the Difference Makes All the Difference

OUR JOB

MICHAEL WM. SCHICK

*"Man fancies himself to be what he is not. He fancies
himself to be God, yet he is only nature, a created being.
From within that illusion he begins to claim for himself
the traits that are the marks of God."*

MARTIN LUTHER

credo
house publishers

To my wife, Diana,
my best friend and the true author of the family,
and my precious daughters, Tiffany and Jessica.
These are my three "Schicklettes" who made
it possible for me to be called "Dad."
I love each of you
more than life itself.

CONTENTS

PREFACE

> *"I have made two important discoveries:
> first, there is a God; second, I'm not him."*

This quip, while humorous in its delivery, is amazingly profound in its essence. With a culture that increasingly encourages self-absorption, it's not surprising that many people act like "little gods" who are confused about their role in life versus God's role over all of life.

While many well-meaning men and women may believe in God, there is a tendency to usurp his function. People try to act like God all the time, attempting in their own power to achieve that which only God alone can accomplish. We try to control circumstances, manipulate situations, prevent mishaps, redefine morality, exalt ourselves or avoid the inevitable. In the end, we must face reality: we are mere mortals who are limited, finite and powerless. We do a lousy job of playing God, and the sooner we realize this, the better.

It is not my intention to write a book about God's attributes, as there are already many great classics that brilliantly address the nature and character of God by looking at *who God is*. Instead, this book is focused on *what God does* and what we are to do accordingly.

Our society glorifies self-sufficiency, intellectual prowess, personal achievement, creative genius and survivor instincts. We are told to "just do it," but *do* what? And for what purpose?

In the 1980s movie *Chariots of Fire*, Olympic runner Eric Liddell shares a key observation with his sister: "God made me fast, and when I run I feel his pleasure." I believe there is pleasure in doing what God made us to do. And while he hasn't made us all with the same gifts, each of us has the same job in light of his job.

A monk once overheard St. Francis of Assisi repeatedly praying, "O God, who are you, and who am I?" In a similar fashion, we might do well to pray, "O God, what are you doing in the world, and what am I supposed to do?" Or, more precisely, "What is your job, and what is my job?"

I would be naïve and arrogant to think this simple book could even scratch the surface of the infinite activities of God in his universe. But I do believe the Scriptures give us an exciting glimpse into what he's working on as he unfolds his divine plan for his most-prized creation, his image bearers—people just like you.

As you read through these thirty-one thoughts, I pray that you come away with a greater appreciation for God's wonderful, majestic and loving acts that are all done with you and your best interests in mind. In return, may you have the ability to do your part as an act of genuine gratitude and worship.

Michael Wm. Schick
Reston, Virginia
January 2013

GOD'S JOB: CREATE
OUR JOB: PRESERVE

Darwinists will tell you that life evolved from very simple cells a long, long time ago. Ask them where the cells came from and how life began in the first place, and they'll tell you we evolved from some primordial goo, or that aliens put us here. Then ask them where the goo or aliens came from, and they'll admit they don't know. That's because their minds know it's impossible for something to come from nothing, and there has been no answer to how simple cells came alive. In their hearts, surely they must know that the effect had a cause . . . the universe had an intelligent designer . . . the creation had a creator. The Bible makes it clear that God made everything ex nihilo (out of nothing), and it was good. Indeed, God did a very good job.

One of the first items on mankind's job description was to care for God's magnificent world. We are to be stewards of it. It is his world, and we its temporary visitors. We don't own it or control it. But we are charged to manage and care for it, which is why we have to protect the land, sky and waters.

Earth truly is a privileged planet. Scientists tell us that it's highly unlikely that a similar planet exists anywhere else in the universe. Earth is all we've got. That's why we must preserve God's creation. Not to do so would be to show him contempt, not to mention jeopardize the future habitability of this wonderful world. So we need to handle God's creation with care. Earth is precious to God and every living creature.

"*Because God created the Natural—invented it out of His love and artistry—it demands our reverence.*"

C. S. LEWIS

GOD'S WORD

GENESIS 1:1 (NLT)   In the beginning God created the heavens and the earth.

JOHN 1:3   Through him all things were made; without him nothing was made that has been made.

PSALM 115:16 (NLT)   The heavens belong to the LORD, but he has given the earth to all humanity.

GENESIS 2:15 (NLT)   The LORD God placed the man in the Garden of Eden to tend and watch over it.

PSALM 24:1 (NLT)   The earth is the LORD's, and everything in it. The world and all its people belong to him.

JOB APPLICATION

1. What are some practical ways you can care for creation?

2. Since God owns everything, what should your perspective be?

3. When does caring for God's creation get out of balance?

GOD'S JOB: REVEAL
OUR JOB: DISCOVER

One of the traditions of Easter Sunday is the egg hunt whereby excited and energetic children scurry about in search of brightly colored eggs hidden by the grownups. Some are placed in easy to find locations, and others require the help of a mom or dad giving the kiddies a hint on where they might be. Some eggs still haven't been found to this day.

Life is like the ultimate hunt. God has many hidden mysteries, and yet he also intends for mankind to constantly make new discoveries. Did man invent gravity, electricity, relativity, thermodynamics or even cures to Polio and other diseases? No, humans merely uncovered them. God revealed them to the seeker.

As much as we'd like to take credit for our diligent searches, the Almighty always has a hand in helping us discover all kinds of truths. We can be glad that he shares our joy when men and women uncover amazing new facts and artifacts. It's all a part of his plan to use human ingenuity to benefit mankind.

"I do not know what I may appear to the world, but to myself I seem to have been only like a boy playing on the sea-shore, and diverting myself in now and then finding a smoother pebble or a prettier shell than ordinary, whilst the great ocean of truth lay all undiscovered before me."

SIR ISAAC NEWTON

GOD'S WORD

JOB 12:22 (NLT) He uncovers mysteries hidden in darkness; he brings light to the deepest gloom.

ECCLESIASTES 3:11 (NLT) He has made everything beautiful in its time. He has also set eternity in the hearts of men; yet they cannot fathom what God has done from the beginning to end.

DANIEL 2:22 (NLT) He reveals deep and mysterious things and knows what lies hidden in darkness, though he is surrounded by light.

DEUTERONOMY 29:29 The secret things belong to the LORD our God, but the things revealed belong to us and to our children forever, that we may follow all the words of this law.

1 CORINTHIANS 2:10 (NLT) But it was to us that God revealed these things by his Spirit. For his Spirit searches out everything and shows us God's deep secrets.

JOB APPLICATION

1. Name some examples of discoveries that have benefitted you?

2. What mysteries would you like God to reveal to you?

3. Take a moment to thank God for specific revelations in your life.

GOD'S JOB: DECLARE
OUR JOB: PROCLAIM

With all due respect, God is a show-off. It is entirely his right to draw our attention to himself. After all, he made everything for his glory and our enjoyment. The Psalmist says, "The heavens declare the glory of God," (Psalm 19:1). As astronomers discover new and amazing wonders in the deep recesses of space using the latest technologies and powerful telescopes, we see more and more of God's awesome handiwork in resplendent majesty. The same is true when we peer into powerful microscopes and see the extraordinary and intricate details of the cellular world. God uses all these telescopic and microscopic instruments as mere visual aids to declare the reality of his incomprehensible greatness.

His job is to display the magnificent grandeur of his divine nature for all to see. Our job is to proclaim the wonders of our Creator to a world desperately searching for meaning, purpose and destiny. After we invite others to look up to the heavens to see God's craftsmanship filling deep space, we should then invite them to look within their hearts to see the deep void that only an infinite God can fill. And when they find him, they, too, will proclaim his glory. So then, both God's creation and God's creatures will bear witness to the Maker of heaven and earth.

*"Each of us is under
a divine mandate to become
an amateur astronomer,
to peer into the incalculable depths
of sky and space to behold
the handiwork of our
omnipotent Creator."*

SAM STORMS

GOD'S WORD

PSALM 19:1 The heavens declare the glory of God; the skies proclaim the work of his hands.

ISAIAH 40:22, 26 He stretches out the heavens like a canopy, and spreads them out like a tent to live in. . . . Lift up your eyes and look to the heavens: Who created all these? He who brings out the starry host one by one and calls them each by name.

PSALM 96:3 Declare his glory among the nations, his marvelous deeds among all peoples.

PSALM 71:8 My mouth is filled with your praise, declaring your splendor all day long.

ACTS 18:9 (NLT) One night the Lord spoke to Paul in a vision and told him, "Don't be afraid! Speak out! Don't be silent!"

JOB APPLICATION

1. Which marvels of creation remind you of God's majesty?

2. What does God say to you about himself through the wonders of nature?

3. What do you think God wants you to declare to those around you?

GOD'S JOB: SANCTIFY
OUR JOB: GLORIFY

Many people believe that humanity is getting better with each passing day. Nothing could be further from the truth. If anything, we are getting worse with each step away from God and toward self-sufficiency. The Bible says "our righteousness is as filthy rags." In other words, our efforts to be and do good in our own power utterly miss the mark of God's perfect standard. Even a godly man like the apostle Paul said that all his good works and noble achievements amounted to nothing more than "dung" in comparison to knowing Christ.

Since we are so spiritually dirty, it's up to God to wash us because we are incapable of cleaning up ourselves. This supernatural cleansing from our disgusting nature is called sanctification, the process of making us clean and spotless. Isaiah 1:18 says, "Though your sins are like scarlet, they shall be as white as snow; though they be red as crimson, they shall be like wool." How? Through the precious blood of Jesus Christ, "the Lamb of God, who takes away the sins of the world." (John 1:29) Jesus made it his job to die in our place so that we would be clean enough to enter God's presence. Our job, in return, is to glorify him by showing the world our new, fresh and clean heart.

*"Man's chief end
is to glorify God,
and to enjoy him forever."*

WESTMINSTER
SHORTER CATECHISM

GOD'S WORD

ISAIAH 1:18 "Come now, let us settle the matter," says the LORD. "Though your sins are like scarlet, they shall be as white as snow; though they are red as crimson, they shall be like wool."

1 CORINTHIANS 6:11 You were washed, you were sanctified, you were justified in the name of the Lord Jesus Christ and by the Spirit of our God.

1 JOHN 1:7 (NASB) But if we walk in the Light as He Himself is in the Light, we have fellowship with one another, and the blood of Jesus His Son cleanses us from all sin.

1 THESSALONIANS 5:23 May God himself, the God of peace, sanctify you through and through. May your whole spirit, soul and body be kept blameless at the coming of our Lord Jesus Christ.

1 CORINTHIANS 6:20 (NASB) For you have been bought with a price; therefore glorify God in your body.

JOB APPLICATION

1. Make a mental list of your failures, then invite Christ to erase them.

2. What are some ways to keep yourself "clean" in a "dirty" world?

3. Name some ways you can glorify God.

GOD'S JOB: HOLD TOGETHER
OUR JOB: HOLD ON

Scientists tell us that everything is made up of molecules that aren't even touching. Things that appear solid, including you and me, aren't really solid at all. They are held together by electromagnetism. Thanks to gravity, the stars and planets are suspended in space at precisely the right places. So what holds gravity and electromagnetism together? God. Colossians 1:16-17 says Christ created all things and "in him all things hold together." If he were to let go, all things would implode, explode and disintegrate.

God's job is to hold it all together. If he can be trusted to hold the universe together, we can trust him to hold us together—even when our lives seem to be falling apart. Our journey through life will be a bumpy road, with trials and tragedies threatening to undo us. Cling to God like your life depends on it, because it does. Hold on to God and don't let go. And even if you do lose your grip, he won't. As Jesus said in John 10:28, nothing can snatch his followers from his hand. There is no safer place than being in his hands.

"So for us, the condition and
preparation on and by which
we are sheltered by that great hand,
is the faith that asks,
and the asking of faith.
We must forsake the earthly props,
but we must also believingly desire
to be upheld by the heavenly arms.
We make God responsible
for our safety when we abandon
other defense, and commit
ourselves to Him."

ALEXANDER MACLAREN

GOD'S WORD

COLOSSIANS 1:17 (NLT) [Jesus] existed before anything else, and he holds all creation together.

ISAIAH 42:6 (NLT) "I, the LORD, have called you to demonstrate my righteousness. I will take you by the hand and guard you."

PSALM 63:8 (NLT) I cling to you; your strong right hand holds me securely.

PSALM 37:24 (NLT) Though they stumble, they will never fall, for the LORD holds them by the hand.

JOHN 10:28 "I give them eternal life, and they shall never perish; no one will snatch them out of my hand."

JOB APPLICATION

1. How does it make you feel to know Christ holds you securely?

2. Are there areas of your life you still cling to instead of trusting Christ with them?

3. By faith, visualize putting all you hold dear in God's hands.

GOD'S JOB: REIGN
OUR JOB: SERVE

For nearly 1,000 years, much of mankind embraced the Ptole-maic or "geocentric" view of the solar system: namely that the earth was at the center, and the sun, moon, stars and planets orbited around it. By the late sixteenth century, however, this belief was replaced by the "heliocentric" model of Copernicus, Galileo and Kepler, which put the sun, not earth, at the center. Later, scientific discovery revealed the incomprehensible dis-tances and magnitude of outer space.

It is not uncommon for people today to act Ptolemaic in that they believe they are at the center of their world and that everything and everyone revolves around them. They want or expect others, including God, to serve or cater to them. The eventual chaos that emanates from this self-centered attitude can only be reordered when we replace ourselves with Christ at the center of our lives. He alone reigns as the undisputed Master of the universe. His job isn't to serve us; our job is to serve him.

Our precisely designed solar system operates so magnif-icently because God put the sun at the center in its rightful place. Our personal world will likewise function best when we, as servants, put the Son of God at the center in his rightful place as the Lord who reigns sovereignly over all.

"God is not greater
if you reverence Him,
but you are greater
if you serve Him."

AUGUSTINE

GOD'S WORD

PSALM 97:1 The LORD reigns, let the earth be glad; let the distant shores rejoice.

PSALM 2:11 (NLT) Serve the LORD with reverent fear, and rejoice with trembling.

PSALM 100:2 (NASB) Serve the LORD with gladness; Come before Him with joyful singing.

PSALM 99:1–2 The LORD reigns, let the nations tremble; he sits enthroned between the cherubim, let the earth shake. Great is the LORD in Zion; he is exalted over all the nations.

ISAIAH 40:22 He sits enthroned above the circle of the earth, and its people are like grasshoppers. He stretches out the heavens like a canopy, and spreads them out like a tent to live in.

EXODUS 15:18 (NLT) The LORD will reign forever and ever!

JOB APPLICATION

1. Who is the center of your life? God? You? Someone or something else?

2. What have been results of this focus?

3. What are some realistic ways you can serve God as your personal king?

GOD'S JOB: CONTROL
OUR JOB: SURRENDER

God is sovereign. He is in complete control. This truth is hard to comprehend when tragedy strikes, when we lose a loved one or when we suffer great pain or injustice. We might catch ourselves saying, "If I were God, I would do things differently."

In the book of Job, Job complained to God. But Job wasn't quite ready for God's answer in Job 38. "Brace yourself like a man," God told him. "Where were you when I brought creation into being? Do you tell the ocean you can go this far to the land but no further? Do the lightning bolts report to you, saying 'here we are?'"

God knows what he is doing. He is perfectly able to take all the mess that man has caused and experienced in this fallen world and work it together for our good and his glory. Genesis 37 records how Joseph was sold by his brothers into slavery in Egypt where he ended up in prison for years. But as only he can, God exalted Joseph from prisoner to being Pharaoh's prime minister and then used Joseph's power and influence to save Israel from extinction during a famine. Joseph was able to declare to his brothers that what they meant for evil, God meant for good, for a higher purpose.

Nothing is too great for God; he is in charge of everything. Christ stopped the storm with a mere command, "Peace, be still." When we surrender to his control, we will, like the stormy sea, be at peace.

"What you need to do,
is to put your will over completely
into the hands of your Lord,
surrendering to Him the entire
control of it. Say, "Yes, Lord, YES!"
to everything, and trust Him
to work in you to will,
as to bring your whole wishes
and affections into conformity
with His own sweet,
and lovable, and most lovely will."

HANNAH WHITALL SMITH

GOD'S WORD

MARK 4:37–41 (NLT) But soon a fierce storm came up. High waves were breaking into the boat, and it began to fill with water . . . . When Jesus woke up, he rebuked the wind and said to the waves, "Silence! Be still!" Suddenly the wind stopped, and there was a great calm. Then he asked them, "Why are you afraid? Do you still have no faith?" The disciples were absolutely terrified. "Who is this man?" they asked each other. "Even the wind and waves obey him!"

JOB 37:15 (NLT) Do you know how God controls the storm and causes the lightning to flash from his clouds?

JEREMIAH 10:23 (NLT) I know, LORD, that our lives are not our own. We are not able to plan our own course.

ROMANS 8:28 (NLT) And we know that God causes everything to work together for the good of those who love God and are called according to his purpose for them.

JOB APPLICATION

1. What events in your life appeared like God was not in control?

2. God's control doesn't mean he causes bad things. What are some causes of evil in our world?

3. What specific matters do you need to surrender to God's control?

GOD'S JOB: SEEK
OUR JOB: SEEK

You may have heard someone say, "I found God," as if he were lost or hiding. The truth is, God finds us first. Jesus said that he came to earth "to seek and save the lost." His parables demonstrate this truth—from the shepherd who left the ninety-nine sheep to find the one lost sheep to the widow who lost a coin and searched until she found it. These stories refer to God's initiative, not ours. The Lord says, "He who seeks me will surely find me, when he seeks me with all his heart." Amazingly, those of us who have sought the truth and discovered it in Christ eventually learn this phenomenal principle—that he was orchestrating our paths toward himself. He gave us the very urge to seek him. He gave us the gift of repentance, enabling us to turn from sin and toward him. He gave us the gift of faith to believe in him. So now, as his children, he tells us to seek first his kingdom and his righteousness and everything else we need will be given to us. Thank God that he loved us enough to seek us out first. What a comfort to know that our search for truth begins and ends with him— the Author and Finisher of our faith.

"Thou didst seek us
when we sought Thee not;
didst seek us indeed
that we might seek Thee."

AUGUSTINE

GOD'S WORD

LUKE 19:10 (NLT) "For the Son of Man came to seek and save those who are lost."

MATTHEW 6:33 (NLT) "Seek the Kingdom of God above all else, and live righteously, and he will give you everything you need."

1 JOHN 4:10 This is love: not that we loved God, but that he loved us and sent his Son as an atoning sacrifice for our sins.

JEREMIAH 29:13 "You will seek me and find me when you seek me with all your heart."

JAMES 4:8 Come near to God and he will come near to you.

PSALM 27:8 My heart says of you, "Seek his face!" Your face, LORD, I will seek.

PSALM 105:4 (NLT) Search for the LORD and for his strength; continually seek him.

ZEPHANIAH 2:3 (NLT) Seek the LORD, all who are humble, and follow his commands. Seek to do what is right and to live humbly.

JOB APPLICATION

1. What does it mean to you that God is pursuing a relation-
    ship with you?

2. What happens when you seek God before all else?

3. What part does God have in your search for truth, mean-
    ing and purpose?

GOD'S JOB: KNOW ALL
OUR JOB: KNOW GOD

God is omniscient. His job is to know everything. He knows
the deep past and the most distant future. There is nothing
he doesn't know. We, on the other hand, know very little in
comparison. It's humbling, to be sure, but it's also comforting
and freeing to realize that God knows all and we don't have
to. Quite frankly, we couldn't handle it.

Our job is to know the One who knows it all—God.
We would do well to follow the same precepts established
in the seventeenth century by that great Ivy League pillar of
knowledge—Harvard University—namely ". . . to know God
and Jesus Christ, which is eternal life." That's really all you
need to know, for when you know Jesus—not just know about
him—but have a personal relationship with him, you will
know the one who loves you and gave his life for you.

The apostle Paul, one of history's most brilliant men,
summed it up best when he said, "Knowledge puffs up, but
love builds up." (1 Corinthians 8:1) When we know God
more and more, we will love him more and more. We will
also love others more purely. Who cares how smart you are?
What matters is how loving you are, and that starts by knowing God.

"I am graven on the palms
of His hands. I am never
out of His mind. All my knowledge
of Him depends on His sustained
initiative in knowing me.
I know Him, because He first
knew me, and continues to know me.
He knows me as a friend,
One who loves me; and there
is no moment when His eye is off me,
or His attention distracted
from me, and no moment, therefore,
when His care falters."

J. I. PACKER

GOD'S WORD

PSALM 94:11 The LORD knows all human plans; he knows that they are futile.

PSALM 139:1, 4 You have searched me, LORD, and you know me. . . . Before a word is on my tongue you, LORD, know it completely.

JOHN 17:3 "Now this is eternal life: that they know you, the only true God, and Jesus Christ, whom you have sent."

1 CORINTHIANS 2:2 For I resolved to know nothing while I was with you except Jesus Christ and him crucified.

1 CORINTHIANS 8:1 We know that "We all possess knowledge." But knowledge puffs up while love builds up.

COLOSSIANS 2:2–3 My goal is that they may be encouraged in heart and united in love, so that they may have the full riches of complete understanding, in order that they may know the mystery of God, namely, Christ, in whom are hidden all the treasures of wisdom and knowledge.

JOB APPLICATION

1. Compare your knowledge with God's. How does that make you feel?

2. What does it mean to you to know the Lord personally?

3. What is it like realizing that you are always on God's mind?

GOD'S JOB: REDEEM
OUR JOB: RECEIVE

Most world religions operate under the premise that a person must be good to earn his way to heaven or some other eternal reward. Under this "works" system, the onus is literally "on us" to be the agent of salvation. The Christian faith, however, is radically different. It concedes that mankind is in big trouble spiritually. Romans 3:10 tells us "There is no one righteous," meaning that no one is good enough to win God's favor. Furthermore, God is perfect, and no imperfect person can enter his heaven. We can't save ourselves; we need help from someone able to rescue us.

Jesus, God's Son, is the only one good enough to bring salvation to humanity. With his own sinless and perfect life, Jesus paid the ransom to free us. Thus, he chose to redeem us, purchasing our redemption with his own blood, so that we can live in heaven forever. That was his job as Redeemer. In response to this unfathomable sacrifice, all we have to do is receive this great and wonderful and precious gift. If you want to know God personally, to become his child and live forever in glory with him and his family, simply receive the gift of eternal life that only the great redeemer can give.

*"My memory is nearly gone,
but I remember two things:
that I am a great sinner,
and that Christ is a great Savior."*

JOHN NEWTON

GOD'S WORD

JOHN 3:16–17 For God so loved the world that he gave his one and only Son, that whoever believes in him shall not perish but have eternal life. For God did not send his Son into the world to condemn the world, but to save the world through him.

JOHN 5:24 "Very truly I tell you, whoever hears my word and believes him who sent me has eternal life and will not be judged but has crossed over from death to life."

JOHN 1:12 Yet to all who did receive him, to those who believed in his name, he gave the right to become children of God.

TITUS 3:5 (NLT) He saved us, not because of the righteous things we had done, but because of his mercy. He washed away our sins, giving us a new birth and new life through the Holy Spirit.

EPHESIANS 2:8–9 For it is by grace you have been saved, through faith—and this not from yourselves, it is the gift of God—not by works, so that no one can boast.

JOB APPLICATION

1. Why can't human beings earn their way to heaven?

2. How is the Christian faith different from all other belief systems?

3. Have you received the eternal gift God bought with his son's life?

GOD'S JOB: LIBERATE
OUR JOB: APPRECIATE

The Bible tells us that by nature we are slaves to sin. We do what is contrary to the nature and character of God. The apostle Paul describes us as people with the habit of "gratifying the cravings of our sinful nature and following its desires and thoughts." Because of this propensity, or, as John Calvin called it "depravity," we were born "objects of wrath." But even though we were previously "dead in our transgressions and sins," God, who is rich in mercy, made those who put their faith in Jesus Christ come alive. Christ has set us free, and as he said, "When the Son of God sets you free, you are free indeed."

Christ has liberated us from our dead and condemned state. That's his job. Our job is to show our undying appreciation by living a life of obedience and service. We follow Christ instead of our old sinful nature. We are no longer slaves to sin, but are now slaves to Christ. As Bob Dylan's gut-honest song puts it, "You can serve the devil or you can serve the Lord, but you gotta serve somebody."

Because Christ has set us free, the least we can do is thank and serve him every day of our lives and, indeed, for all eternity.

"*Long my imprisoned spirit lay,*
fast bound in sin and nature's night;
Thine eye diffused a quickening ray—
I woke, the dungeon flamed with light;
My chains fell off, my heart was free,
I rose, went forth, and followed Thee."

CHARLES WESLEY

GOD'S WORD

JOHN 8:32, 36 (NLT) "And you will know the truth, and the truth will set you free. . . . So if the Son sets you free, you are truly free."

ROMANS 6:18 (NLT) Now you are free from your slavery to sin, and you have become slaves to righteous living.

GALATIANS 4:5 (NLT) God sent [Jesus] to buy freedom for us who were slaves to the law, so that he could adopt us as his very own children.

ROMANS 8:2 (NLT) And because you belong to him, the power of the life-giving Spirit has freed you from the power of sin that leads to death.

REVELATION 1:5 (NLT) All glory to him who loves us and has freed us from our sins by shedding his blood for us.

2 CORINTHIANS 3:17 (NLT) For the Lord is the Spirit, and wherever the Spirit of the Lord is, there is freedom.

PSALM 118:5 (NLT) In my distress I prayed to the Lord, and the Lord answered me and set me free.

PSALM 107:1 Give thanks to the Lord, for he is good; his love endures forever.

PSALM 9:1 (NRSV) I will give thanks to the Lord with my whole heart; I will recount all of your wonderful deeds.

JOB APPLICATION

1. How can you be set free from bondage to sin and spiritual death?

2. From what manner of bondage do you yearn to be set free?

3. How should you respond to Jesus Christ for liberating you?

GOD'S JOB: TRANSFORM
OUR JOB: CONFORM

Thousands of self-help books, seminars, courses and programs have been created to help people do one fundamental thing: change. They appeal to a variety of felt needs, from those who want to break an addiction, to those who want to manage stress or lose weight, to those who want to get rich quick. Millions of people are desperately trying to in some way change their current state. Some succeed in their quest; others don't and end up discouraged, defeated or depressed. In the end, even those who overcome realize they can't bring about change alone—they need "a power greater than themselves," as many 12-step programs acknowledge.

Real change is God's job. He's the ultimate transformer. He takes what is dead—us—and makes us alive. When we place our faith in Christ, he rescues us from the dominion of darkness and ushers us into his Kingdom of light. All he asks in return is that we stop conforming to the patterns/values/ways of this world and conform instead to the image of his Son, Jesus Christ. This is not a mere mandate to adhere to a bunch of religious rules. Rather, it is an invitation to model your life after the character of Jesus, while still maintaining your unique individuality. He loves our distinctiveness, and he knows that the real us will become more apparent as we become more like him. God transforms us by making us a new creation, and by the power of the Holy Spirit, we become more like Jesus every day. Now that's real, lasting change!

"God's purpose in redeeming men from sin is not to give them freedom to do as they please but freedom to do as He pleases, which is to live righteously."

JOHN MACARTHUR

GOD'S WORD

COLOSSIANS 2:13 (NLT) You were dead because of your sins and because your sinful nature was not yet cut away. Then God made you alive with Christ, for he forgave all our sins.

2 CORINTHIANS 5:17 (NLT) Anyone who belongs to Christ has become a new person. The old life is gone; a new life has begun!

ROMANS 12:2 (NLT) Don't copy the behavior and customs of this world, but let God transform you into a new person by changing the way you think. Then you will learn to know God's will for you, which is good and pleasing and perfect.

EPHESIANS 5:1–2 (NLT) Imitate God, therefore, in everything you do, because you are his dear children. Live a life filled with love, following the example of Christ. He loved us and offered himself as a sacrifice for us, a pleasing aroma to God.

ROMANS 8:9 (NLT) But you are not controlled by your sinful nature. You are controlled by the Spirit if you have the Spirit of God living in you.

JOB APPLICATION

1. What role models do you pattern your life after? Are they positive or negative?

2. What is the first step in becoming a truly new person?

3. From where does the power come to live like Jesus?

GOD'S JOB: CONVICT
OUR JOB: CONFESS

Since the beginning of time, man has had a conscience. God implanted in each of us an internal awareness of right and wrong. But as creatures with free will, we also have the ability to harden our hearts and dull our minds to this moral compass. But God, in his grace, is far greater than our stubborn insolence. His Holy Spirit convicts us of the wrong we have done or the right we have left undone. We can't conjure up this conviction on our own power. It must come from God, the perfect, holy law-giver. His Holy Spirit gives us the gift of repentance—eyes to see our shortcomings and sensitivity to feel our failure to keep God's perfect standard of right thinking and acting. God's job is to convict.

Our job is to confess. That means we admit that his assessment of our sin (defined as *s*elf *i*ndulgence *n*ow) is correct, and we need his forgiveness and strength to do right. Sin is pretty basic: it means we thought or did what we should not have thought or done, or that we failed to think or do what we should have done. By confessing, we bring our filthy thoughts, unkind words and selfish deeds into the disinfecting sunlight of his holiness. We then claim the blood of Jesus Christ shed on Calvary's cross to wash those sins away.

To keep short accounts with God and maintain a right relationship with him, we should regularly confess our sins to God. We should even share and confess our innermost thoughts to someone we trust. By exhaling the dirty air of sin to God and one another, we can breathe deeply the pure oxygen of Christ's forgiveness and start afresh.

*"The confession
of evil works
is the first beginning
of good works."*

AUGUSTINE

GOD'S WORD

ROMANS 2:15 (NLT)   They demonstrate that God's law is written within them, for their own consciences either accuse them or tell them they are doing what is right.

JUDE 1:15 (NLT)   [God] will convict every person of all the ungodly things they have done and for all the insults that ungodly sinners have spoken against him.

LEVITICUS 5:5 (NLT)   "When you become aware of your guilt in any of these ways, you must confess your sin."

PSALM 32:5 (NLT)   Finally, I confessed all my sins to you and stopped trying to hide my guilt. I said to myself, "I will confess my rebellion to the LORD." And you forgave me! All my guilt is gone.

JAMES 5:16 (NLT)   Confess your sins to each other and pray for each other so that you may be healed. The earnest prayer of a righteous person has great power and produces wonderful results.

1 JOHN 1:9 (NLT)   But if we confess our sins to him, he is faithful and just to forgive us our sins and to cleanse us from all wickedness.

HEBREWS 9:14   How much more, then, will the blood of Christ, who through the eternal Spirit offered himself unblemished to God, cleanse our consciences from acts that lead to death, so that we may serve the living God!

JOB APPLICATION

1. How do all people in all places for all time know right from wrong?

2. Why do you think confession is "good for the soul"?

3. How does confessing our failures to others impact our behavior?

GOD'S JOB: FORGIVE
OUR JOB: FORGIVE

God is gracious, meaning that he gives us blessings we don't deserve. He is also merciful, meaning that he doesn't give us the punishment we rightfully deserve. It is because of these astonishing attributes that God chose to forgive us.

But this forgiveness, while freely offered, is not cheap. God had to pay an unspeakably high price to secure it—the death of his only Son, Jesus. Only Jesus could do what we couldn't possibly do for ourselves. He took God's righteous wrath against our sin on himself as he hung on the cross. There, our sin was imputed, or credited, to him, so that his righteousness could be justly imputed, or credited, to us who believe.

Since God has done an amazing work to purchase our forgiveness, we are expected—indeed commanded—to forgive others. In fact, the Scriptures say that if we don't forgive others, God won't forgive us. It doesn't matter how terribly we've been wronged or harmed; we must forgive. If we don't, we doom ourselves to exist in a miserable state of bondage that eats at us like acid. As the saying goes, being unforgiving is like taking a poison pill and expecting someone else to die. Our refusal to forgive the offense of another doesn't hurt anyone but ourselves. We may have to forgive over and over again for years, even if it's for the same singular offense that happened in the distant past.

The only way we can sincerely and completely forgive is through the powerful assistance of the Holy Spirit as we choose to surrender the matter to God. When we forgive as God forgave us, we can escape the damning pains of past hurts and be free to enjoy all that God has for us in the present and future.

"[It is] cheaper to pardon
than to resent. Forgiveness saves
the expense of anger,
the cost of hatred,
and the waste of spirit."

HANNAH MORE

GOD'S WORD

DANIEL 9:9 "The Lord our God is merciful and forgiving, even though we have rebelled against him."

ISAIAH 43:25 "I, even I, am he who blots out your transgressions, for my own sake, and remembers your sins no more."

PSALM 103:12 As far as the east is from the west, so far has he removed our transgressions from us.

COLOSSIANS 2:13–14 When you were dead in your sins and in the uncircumcision of your flesh, God made you alive with Christ. He forgave us all our sins, having canceled the charge of our legal indebtedness, which stood against us and condemned us; he has taken it away, nailing it to the cross.

MATTHEW 6:14–15 "For if you forgive other people when they sin against you, your heavenly Father will also forgive you. But if you do not forgive others their sins, your Father will not forgive your sins."

EPHESIANS 4:32 (NLT) Instead, be kind to each other, tenderhearted, forgiving one another, just as God through Christ has forgiven you.

COLOSSIANS 3:13 (NLT) Make allowance for each other's faults, and forgive anyone who offends you. Remember, the Lord forgave you, so you must forgive others.

JOB APPLICATION

1. How does unforgiveness hurt us more than the offender?

2. What are the most important reasons why we should forgive others?

3. Who do you need to forgive? Whose forgiveness do you need to ask? Where can you get the power to do this?

GOD'S JOB: ILLUMINATE
OUR JOB: REFLECT

One of God's attributes is light. Scripture calls it "unapproach-able light," meaning that no unholy human can see a holy God and live, just as we can't get too close to the sun without be-ing consumed. The Scripture describes Jesus, the Son of God, as the "light of the world." In him there is no darkness. He is not only light, but he illuminates our minds with the things he wants us to see and know. C. S. Lewis said, "I believe in God like I believe in the sun, not because I can see it, but because of it, all things are seen."

The moon generates no light of its own, and its beauty is totally dependent on the sun's rays. Similarly, no man or woman can be a light in his or her own power, but he or she can reflect God's light in and to a dark world. That light source is the Holy Spirit who indwells every believer in Jesus Christ. He tells us that we are not to hide our light under a bushel, but are to put our lamp (Christ) on a lamp stand so that all may see him through us. The light we reflect guides oth-ers like a search light leading lost airplanes home. It warns them like a lighthouse telling ships to steer clear. It can be like a warm fire to those inflicted by the harsh cold of an uncar-ing world. This light, the light of Jesus, shines in the darkness, and the darkness will never, ever conquer it. May God help us mirror his light so that others may see him and live.

*"All the darkness in the world
cannot extinguish the light
of a single candle."*

FRANCIS OF ASSISI

GOD'S WORD

1 TIMOTHY 6:16   [God] alone is immortal and who lives in unapproachable light, whom no one has seen or can see. To him be honor and might forever. Amen.

1 JOHN 1:5   This is the message we have heard from him and declare to you: God is light; in him there is no darkness at all.

JOHN 1:4–5   In [Christ] was life, and that life was the light of all mankind. The light shines in the darkness, and the darkness has not overcome it.

MATTHEW 5:15–16   "Neither do people light a lamp and put it under a bowl. Instead they put it on its stand, and it gives light to everyone in the house. In the same way, let your light shine before others, that they may see your good deeds and glorify your Father in heaven."

PHILIPPIANS 2:15   . . . so that you may become blameless and pure, children of God without fault in a warped and crooked generation. Then you will shine among them like stars in the sky.

ISAIAH 60:1   "Arise, shine, for your light has come, and the glory of the LORD rises upon you."

JOB APPLICATION

1. List a few real dangers that arise in the absence of light.

2. What dark areas of your life require the light of Jesus?

3. What results when you reflect Christ's light to others?

GOD'S JOB: LEAD
OUR JOB: FOLLOW

Men are often stereotyped as refusing to ask for directions whenever they get lost. The truth is that men are just doing what they are naturally wired to do—lead. But how can anyone lead without knowing where he or she is going or how to get there?

What is true in driving is also true in life. We are all on a journey, and most of us hope it ends up in a happy place called heaven. Jesus is God incarnate, the One who came from heaven to show us how to get to heaven. He didn't just make the map to heaven; he *is* the map and *the* way. Jesus didn't say "follow my directions," but "follow me." He is the only vehicle capable of transporting us to our destination. And Jesus doesn't just want to lead us to heaven, but he wants to lead us through our daily lives here on earth. He is ready and eager to guide us moment by moment if we will just let him.

How silly to think we know the way on our own. No wonder we are lost. Thank God Jesus came to seek and save the lost. With his direction, we will find the right college, job, spouse, doctor and guidance for any other significant life decisions. Most importantly, we will arrive safely at our ultimate destination—our home in heaven with him.

"We learn about guidance primarily by learning about the Guide. It is the knowledge of God and His ways with men which ultimately gives us stability in doing His will."

SINCLAIR B. FERGUSON

GOD'S WORD

JOHN 14:6 Jesus answered, "I am the way and the truth and the life. No one comes to the Father except through me."

PROVERBS 3:5–6 Trust in the LORD with all your heart and lean not on your own understanding; in all your ways submit to him, and he will make your paths straight.

ISAIAH 30:21 Whether you turn to the right or to the left, your ears will hear a voice behind you, saying, "This is the way; walk in it."

ISAIAH 42:16 "I will lead the blind by ways they have not known, along unfamiliar paths I will guide them; I will turn the darkness into light before them and make the rough places smooth. These are the things I will do; I will not forsake them."

PSALM 32:8 I will instruct you and teach you in the way you should go; I will counsel you with my loving eye on you.

PSALM 73:24 You guide me with your counsel, and afterward you will take me into glory.

PSALM 23:2 He makes me lie down in green pastures, he leads me beside quiet waters.

JOB APPLICATION

1. What wrong turns in your life were caused by following terrible directions?

2. Where do you need God's guidance for your life today?

3. What's the difference in following Jesus and not just his teachings?

GOD'S JOB: ANSWER
OUR JOB: ASK

Why is it that Santa Claus has so much magical appeal? Simple. We ask for something and he delivers. Literally. People have a similar attitude toward God. They want to use him as a divine vending machine; put your prayer in and out comes exactly what you desire.

Here's the fact of the matter: God does hear the prayers of everyone in the world, and he answers everyone's prayer one way or another. But God is under no compulsion to give anyone whatever he asks for. Sometimes his answer to our request is "no," "not now" or "not this." The more important truth is that God answers the prayer of the person who truly seeks his face, not just the gifts of his hands. He loves to give to those who want to be in relationship to him. Would you answer an email, letter or text message from someone you didn't know? God has promised to answer the prayers of his children and those who earnestly seek him.

He always answers, even if we don't understand his answer. But he always answers with a plan that acts in our best interests. Trust him that he knows what he is doing and that you will be better for it, regardless of which answer he gives.

"It is not enough to begin to pray,
nor to pray aright; nor is it enough
to continue for a time to pray;
but we must patiently,
believingly, continue in prayer
until we obtain an answer."

GEORGE MÜLLER

GOD'S WORD

PSALM 34:4 (NLT)   I prayed to the LORD, and he answered me.
He freed me from all my fears.

MATTHEW 7:7–11   "Ask and it will be given to you; seek and you
will find; knock and the door will be opened to you. For
everyone who asks receives; the one who seeks finds; and
to the one who knocks, the door will be opened. Which of
you, if his son asks for bread, will give him a stone? Or if he
asks for a fish, will give him a snake? If you, then, though
you are evil, know how to give good gifts to your children,
how much more will your Father in heaven give good gifts
to those who ask him!"

JOHN 14:13   "And I will do whatever you ask in my name, so that
the Father may be glorified in the Son."

JOHN 15:7   "If you remain in me and my words remain in you,
ask whatever you wish, and it will be done for you."

PHILIPPIANS 4:6–7   Do not be anxious about anything, but in every
situation, by prayer and petition, with thanksgiving, present
your requests to God. And the peace of God, which transcends
all understanding, will guard your hearts and your minds
in Christ Jesus.

1 JOHN 5:14–15   This is the confidence we have in approaching
God: that if we ask anything according to his will, he hears
us. And if we know that he hears us—whatever we ask—we
know that we have what we asked of him.

JOB APPLICATION

1. What obstacles keep you from praying?

2. What does it mean if God doesn't give you what you want?

3. If we are afraid, worried or anxious, how can prayer help?

GOD'S JOB: EXALT
OUR JOB: HUMBLE OURSELVES

There is no place on earth quite like Washington, DC. It is a town filled with very powerful people—a city that attracts the best and brightest, men and women who are hungry for power, prestige, recognition, influence and acclaim. As people calculate and execute their upward ascent strategies, many are convinced that they will be happy when they reach the very pinnacle of success. But they are in for a rude awakening, because those who climb aggressively to the top, those who raise themselves above others, are headed for a great fall. The Scriptures promise that "he who exalts himself shall be humbled, but whoever humbles himself shall be exalted."

It seems so counterintuitive, but Jesus said that the way to greatness is by becoming a servant, not a star. If you really want to become somebody, then don't be afraid to be a "nobody." Your role model is none other than Jesus himself. Though he was God, he humbled himself and thought only in terms of serving God and others. As a result, God exalted him above every throne and dominion. If Jesus humbled himself, should we not, as well? When we humble ourselves, God lifts us up to heights we never could have attained by our own striving. Jesus, the Son of God, humbled himself. Should we not do likewise?

"Power is given only to those who dare to lower themselves. . . . Only one thing matters, one thing; to be able to dare!"

FYODOR DOSTOEVSKY

GOD'S WORD

PROVERBS 11:2 (NLT) Pride leads to disgrace, but with humility comes wisdom.

MATTHEW 23:12 (NLT) "But those who exalt themselves will be humbled, and those who humble themselves will be exalted."

1 PETER 5:6–7 (NLT) So humble yourselves under the mighty power of God, and at the right time he will lift you up in honor. Give all your worries and cares to God, for he cares about you.

PHILIPPIANS 2:3–4 (NLT) Don't be selfish; don't try to impress others. Be humble, thinking of others as better than yourselves. Don't look out only for your own interests, but take an interest in others, too.

PHILIPPIANS 2:5–9 Have the same mindset as Christ Jesus: Who, being in very nature God, did not consider equality with God something to be used to his own advantage; rather, he made himself nothing, by taking the very nature of a servant, being made in human likeness. . . . He humbled himself by becoming obedient to death—even death on a cross! Therefore, God exalted him to the highest place and gave him the name that is above every name.

LUKE 1:51–52 (NLT) His mighty arm has done tremendous things! He has scattered the proud and haughty ones. He has brought down princes from their thrones and exalted the humble.

JOB APPLICATION

1. What ways have you been tempted to exalt yourself in your particular world?

2. What does Jesus' example of humility challenge you to do?

3. What are some benefits of putting God and others before yourself?

GOD'S JOB: DELIVER
OUR JOB: WAIT

If you have never been in a tough situation before, just wait; you will be. And you will likely cry out for God to help you. David, as a shepherd and then a king, found himself in tight spots all the time, and he instinctively cried out for God to deliver him. God will provide deliverance or a way of escape, but it may not come immediately or in the form we expect. That's because God wants to teach us something in the process of waiting—namely, patience. It's not that God is slow; it's that we are in too big of a hurry. We want what we want when we want it.

God knows best. Because of his love for us, he will not intervene until we've learned the lessons we need to know, even if it's not pleasant. Superman, Spiderman and all the other super heroes won't sweep in to save us, because they don't exist. But God really does exist, and he will show up and never be late. If you ever wonder, rest assured that God will rescue you in due time. Just wait and see.

"What then are we to do
about our problems?
We must learn to live with them
until such time as God delivers us
from them. . . . We must pray
for grace to endure them
without murmuring. Problems
patiently endured will work for
our spiritual perfecting. They
harm us only when we resist them
or endure them unwillingly."

A. W. TOZER

GOD'S WORD

PSALM 37:7   Be still before the Lord and wait patiently for him.

PSALM 46:1   God is our refuge and strength, an ever-present help in trouble.

PSALM 91:14   "Because he loves me," says the Lord, "I will rescue him; I will protect him, for he acknowledges my name."

ISAIAH 40:31 (NASB)   Yet those who wait for the Lord will gain new strength; They will mount up with wings like eagles, they will run and not get tired, they will walk and not become weary.

1 CORINTHIANS 10:13 (NLT)   The temptations in your life are no different from what others experience. And God is faithful. He will not allow the temptation to be more than you can stand. When you are tempted, he will show you a way out so that you can endure.

HEBREWS 13:6   So we say with confidence, "The Lord is my helper; I will not be afraid. What can mere mortals do to me?"

JAMES 1:3–4 (NLT)   For when your faith is tested, your endurance has a chance to grow. So let it grow, for when your endurance is fully developed, you will be strong in character and ready for anything.

JOB APPLICATION

1. What happens when you are impatient for God to work?

2. What does God's Word promise if we call on him to deliver us from trials or temptations?

3. Why is it liberating to know that God will be faithful to rescue you?

GOD'S JOB: AVENGE
OUR JOB: DEFER

During a family vacation in the Caribbean, I was robbed twice in three days. The first theft happened at night when someone stole my favorite sandals. A few days later at a different location, someone stole my beach bag in broad daylight. The crooks made off with a video camera, my wife's watch, several articles of clothing and other valuables. I felt pretty violated the first time, but the second time really made me angry. I felt justified in wanting to punish the culprits. My wife told me to let it go, reminding me that someone must have needed those things more than I did.

I'll never know who wronged me, but what do you do when someone you do know has hurt you or a loved one? If you are like me, you want to get even. But the Scriptures warn us that revenge is God's job, not ours. If the offense was especially egregious, the legal system is in place to render justice. But even if it's beyond anything the courts can remedy, taking matters into our own hands won't work. It will most likely only make matters worse. Whatever offense you've experienced, put it in God's hands. With perfect justice, he will handle it far better than we ever can.

"Revenge . . . is like a rolling stone,
which, when a man hath forced
up a hill, will return upon him
with a greater violence,
and break those bones whose sinews
gave it motion."

ALBERT SCHWEITZER

GOD'S WORD

ROMANS 12:19 (NLT) Dear friends, never take revenge. Leave that to the righteous anger of God. For the Scriptures say, "I will take revenge; I will pay them back," says the LORD.

PROVERBS 20:22 (NLT) Don't say, "I will get even for this wrong." Wait for the LORD to handle the matter.

LEVITICUS 19:18 (NLT) "Do not seek revenge or bear a grudge against [another]."

MATTHEW 5:39 (NLT) "But I say, do not resist an evil person! If someone slaps you on the right cheek, offer the other cheek also."

PSALM 37:8 (NLT) Stop being angry! Turn from your rage! Do not lose your temper—it only leads to harm.

JOB APPLICATION

1. What happens when you try to get even with somebody?

2. Why is it better to let God take revenge on your behalf?

3. What can you do to resist the temptation to retaliate?

GOD'S JOB: PROVIDE
OUR JOB: PRAISE

In the movie *Shenandoah*, Jimmy Stewart plays Charlie Anderson, a wealthy rancher/farmer in Virginia. At dinner each night, Anderson prays, "Lord, we cleared this land. We plowed it, sowed it and harvested it. We cooked the harvest. It wouldn't be here and we wouldn't be eating it if we hadn't done it all ourselves. We worked dog-bone hard for every crumb and morsel, but we thank you just the same anyway, Lord, for this food we're about to eat. Amen."

What Anderson missed is how God provided the seed, soil, rain and sun—everything that is required to make Anderson's crops grow in the first place. Abraham called God "Jehovah Jireh," meaning "the LORD provides," after God graciously spared his son Isaac and substituted a sacrificial lamb in his place. Later, God did not spare his own son, Jesus, but provided him as the once-and-for-all sacrifice to atone for our sins. God's job is to always provide for his children, even when we doubt it and impatiently try to provide for our own needs. Our job is to praise God for all he has given and will give.

God is a good provider. When the solution to your most vexing problem is not apparent, just wait for the Lord. He will provide in his time and his way. And when he does, be sure to praise him.

*"God wants to see prayers
that are filled with genuine
praise and thanksgiving for
what He has done in the past.
He wants our hearts
to be filled with awe and
gratitude for His blessings.
He wants us to set up
memorials in our hearts
testifying to the provisions
He has given us."*

MICHAEL YOUSSEF

GOD'S WORD

GENESIS 22:13–14 (NLT) Then Abraham looked up and saw a ram caught by its horns in a thicket. So he took the ram and sacrificed it as a burnt offering in place of his son. Abraham named the place Jehovah Jireh (which means "the LORD will provide").

1 CHRONICLES 29:14 "But who am I, and who are my people, that we should be able to give as generously as this? Everything comes from you, and we have given you only what comes from your hand."

LUKE 12:24 "Consider the ravens: They do not sow or reap, they have no storeroom or barn; yet God feeds them. And how much more valuable you are than birds!"

MATTHEW 7:11 "If you, then, though you are evil, know how to give good gifts to your children, how much more will your Father in heaven give good gifts to those who ask him!"

PHILIPPIANS 4:19 And my God will meet all your needs according to the riches of his glory in Christ Jesus.

1 TIMOTHY 6:17 Command those who are rich in this present world not to be arrogant nor to put their hope in wealth, which is so uncertain, but to put their hope in God, who richly provides us with everything for our enjoyment.

JAMES 1:17 Every good and perfect gift is from above, coming down from the Father of the heavenly lights.

JOB APPLICATION

1. Who is ultimately responsible for providing for your needs?

2. How can you distinguish wants from needs?

3. What hindrances keep you from praising God?

GOD'S JOB: SEND
OUR JOB: GO

In today's fast-paced world, it's easy to fall victim to the belief that we need to be in constant motion. All too often, highly motivated believers come up with a grand scheme to do some noble work for God. They are so eager that they set their plans in motion and ask God to bless it after the fact.

But that's not how God works. He is the One who makes the first move, not us. He calls; we go. We don't go and ask him to come along. To go first and expect God to follow by blessing us is "ask backwards." He asks, "Whom shall I send? And who will go for us?" We answer, as Isaiah did, "Here am I. Send me!" (Isaiah 6:8) Isaiah was ready to go, and God clearly had a mission for him. Isaiah didn't know what God's assignment was at the time of the calling, but knowing it didn't matter. Being available for God's service to fulfill God's purpose is all that matters. God has a mission for you in this world. Jesus said, "Go and make disciples." Are you ready to go? God will send you at just the right time. Let him make the first move.

"Rest in this—it is
His business to lead, command,
impel, send, call or whatever
you want to call it. It is
your business to obey, follow,
move, respond, or what have you."

JIM ELLIOT

GOD'S WORD

ISAIAH 6:8 Then I heard the voice of the Lord saying, "Whom shall I send? And who will go for us?" And I said, "Here am I. Send me!"

MATTHEW 10:16, 19–20 "I am sending you out like sheep among wolves. Therefore be as shrewd as snakes and as innocent as doves. . . . Do not worry about what to say or how to say it. At that time you will be given what to say, for it will not be you speaking, but the Spirit of your Father speaking through you."

ISAIAH 45:2 "I will go before you and will level the mountains; I will break down gates of bronze and cut through bars of iron."

PSALM 32:8 I will instruct you and teach you in the way you should go; I will counsel you with my loving eye on you.

MATTHEW 28:19–20 "Therefore go and make disciples of all nations, baptizing them in the name of the Father and of the Son and of the Holy Spirit, and teaching them to obey everything I have commanded you. And surely I am with you always, to the very end of the age."

JOB APPLICATION

1. Why do you think we tend to make plans first and then ask God to bless them?

2. What does God want all of his followers to do?

3. Has God clearly called you for some special work? Are you ready to obey his call and step out on faith?

GOD'S JOB: HEAL
OUR JOB: HELP

Thank God for doctors, nurses and all of the dedicated health-care professionals who provide medical care to hurting people. We need them from cradle to grave, and they play a critical role in life. But they do not heal, for only God can heal. They are God's instruments, or as Dr. Richard J. Foster likes to call them, "God's friends, the doctors." Any physician wise and humble enough to speak truth will tell you that he or she doesn't heal, but merely helps. Modern medicines and devices, imaging and surgical techniques have advanced in unimaginable ways. However, it is God who ultimately uses those innovations for our good and his glory.

Since we live in a time when new medical breakthroughs are being made at record speeds, we have come to expect a pill or procedure to always enable us to live better and longer. The truth is that good health and longevity are not a right, but a privilege. We would do well to remember that every beat of our heart and every breath we take is a gift from the Great Physician, Jesus, the Son of God. If we're willing to help, we can be his instruments of healing to a hurting world.

> *"I am a little pencil*
> *in the hand of a writing God*
> *who is sending a love letter*
> *to the world."*

MOTHER TERESA

GOD'S WORD

MATTHEW 8:2–3 (NLT)   Suddenly, a man with leprosy approached him and knelt before him. "Lord," the man said, "if you are willing, you can heal me and make me clean." Jesus reached out and touched him. "I am willing," he said. "Be healed!" And instantly the leprosy disappeared.

1 PETER 2:24 (NLT)   [Jesus] personally carried our sins in his body on the cross so that we can be dead to sin and live for what is right. By his wounds you are healed.

ISAIAH 53:4–5 (NLT)   He took our sicknesses and removed our diseases. And we thought his troubles were a punishment from God, a punishment for his own sins! But he was pierced for our rebellion, crushed for our sins. He was beaten so we could be whole. He was whipped so we could be healed.

JAMES 5:13–15 (NLT)   Are any of you sick? You should call for the elders of the church to come and pray over you, anointing you with oil in the name of the Lord. Such a prayer offered in faith will heal the sick, and the Lord will make you well.

PSALM 103:3   [The Lord is the one] who forgives all your sins and heals all your diseases.

JEREMIAH 30:17   "But I will restore you to health and heal your wounds," declares the LORD.

JOB APPLICATION

1. Who is ultimately responsible for healing us?

2. We can't all be physicians, but how can we help those with physical needs?

3. Since you are healed by the wounds of Jesus, what should you do?

GOD'S JOB: COMFORT
OUR JOB: COMFORT

Life is full of suffering. It's one of the great tragedies of the fall of mankind. We all suffer in one way or another: emotionally, physically or mentally. Our suffering reminds us that we are powerless and limited in our ability to stop the pain. God's job is to comfort us in our sorrow. He may choose to end our pain or discomfort, or he may choose not to for reasons beyond our comprehension. The apostle Paul asked God to remove an area of deep pain from his life, but God said no. However, he did promise to give Paul, and us, his sufficient grace to help us in our weakness.

God is the God of all comfort. Jesus is the Prince of Peace. The Lord is faithful to calm our troubled hearts in the midst of even the greatest heartache or fear. And he calls us to comfort others in need, as well. Those who are strong are to sustain those who are weak. Those who are not hurting are to help those who are. Each one of us will be on either side of this comfort equation at some point in our lives. Jesus says, "Blessed are the merciful, for they shall receive mercy." Indeed, we have already received mercy from God through the gift of Jesus, and he now charges us to show mercy in his name. You may be the only human source of comfort to someone in your life at this very moment. Don't miss this opportunity to be God's agent of care and compassion to a hurting world.

*"If there is any kindness
I can show, or any good thing
I can do to any fellow being,
let me do it now, and not deter
or neglect it, as I shall not
pass this way again."*

WILLIAM PENN

GOD'S WORD

MATTHEW 11:28 (NLT)   Then Jesus said, "Come to me, all of you who are weary and carry heavy burdens, and I will give you rest."

JEREMIAH 31:13 (NLT)   The young women will dance for joy and the men—old and young—will join in the celebration. I will turn their mourning into joy. I will comfort them and exchange their sorrow for rejoicing.

ISAIAH 49:13 (NLT)   Sing for joy, O heavens! Rejoice, O earth! Burst into song, O mountains! For the LORD has comforted his people and will have compassion on them in their suffering.

PSALM 34:18   The LORD is close to the brokenhearted and saves those who are crushed in spirit.

2 CORINTHIANS 1:4 (NLT)   He comforts us in all our troubles so that we can comfort others. When they are troubled, we will be able to give them the same comfort God has given us.

PSALM 23:4 (NLT)   Even when I walk through the darkest valley, I will not be afraid, for you are close beside me. Your rod and your staff protect and comfort me.

JOHN 16:33 (NLT)   "I have told you all this so that you may have peace in me. Here on earth you will have many trials and sorrows. But take heart, because I have overcome the world."

JOB APPLICATION

1. When have you experienced God's comfort?

2. What does it mean to show mercy?

3. List three hurting people you can offer comfort to this week.

GOD'S JOB: PROTECT
OUR JOB: DEFEND

God is protecting us, even when we don't realize it. Only God knows how many times in a given day he has kept us out of harm's way. He may have intervened in a potential accident, or even a deliberate attack by an enemy, seen or unseen. It's easy to take God's protection for granted, especially when we have no idea how close a call we've missed. God's job is to protect us. But sometimes we make decisions that put God to the test, such as doing things we shouldn't. In such cases, God isn't obliged to protect us when we've wandered from the safety zone of his presence and principles, either through foolish defiance or subtle disobedience. In fact, sometimes God lets us experience the consequences of our poor choices now to protect us from a greater harm later. God helps us because he knows we are weak.

Likewise, he calls us to defend the weak and defenseless. That includes the elderly, the young, those with special needs and even the unborn. God is the giver and sustainer of life. As his people, we are to be his ambassadors against the enemies of life. Throughout history, cultures of death have inflicted untold atrocities on men, women and children made in God's image. If we want to be a blessing to society, we must defend those who cannot fight for themselves. Such is the hallmark of the people of God.

*"The test of a civilization
is the way that it cares
for its helpless members."*

PEARL S. BUCK

GOD'S WORD

PSALM 46:1   God is our refuge and strength, an ever-present help in trouble.

ROMANS 8:31   What, then, shall we say in response to these things? If God is for us, who can be against us?

PSALM 121:7–8   The LORD will keep you from all harm—he will watch over your life; the LORD will watch over your coming and going both now and forevermore.

PSALM 138:7   Though I walk in the midst of trouble, you preserve my life. You stretch out your hand against the anger of my foes; with your right hand you save me.

PSALM 32:7   You are my hiding place; you will protect me from trouble and surround me with songs of deliverance.

PROVERBS 18:10   The name of the LORD is a fortified tower; the righteous run to it and are safe.

ROMANS 15:1 (NAS)   Now we who are strong ought to bear the weaknesses of those without strength and not just please ourselves.

MICAH 6:8   He has shown you, O mortal, what is good. And what does the LORD require of you? To act justly and to love mercy and to walk humbly with your God.

HEBREWS 13:3   Remember those in prison as if you were together with them in prison, and those who are mistreated as if you yourselves were suffering.

LUKE 6:36   "Be merciful, just as your Father is merciful."

JOB APPLICATION

1. Can you think of specific examples of how God has protected you?

2. How can you trust God for protection in situations you are facing today?

3. How can you use your strength to defend the helpless?

GOD'S JOB: **LOVE**
OUR JOB: **LOVE**

It is one thing to say, "I love you"; it's quite another to prove it in actions. God didn't just tell us he loves us, but he demonstrated that love by sending Jesus to die in our place. It was the only way a holy God could allow unholy people into fellowship with himself. Jesus spoke of the ultimate sacrifice, saying, "There is no greater love than this, that a person lays down his life for another."

Jesus also commanded us to "love one another as I have loved you." Loving others is not an option, nor is it limited to the lovely or lovable. Jesus tells us to love our enemies—even those who hate us. Nothing is as unnatural and illogical as this directive, but Jesus meant every word. Humanly speaking, he is asking the impossible. Divinely speaking, it's entirely possible. How do prisoners of war forgive their captors? Love. How does a husband forgive his adulterous wife? Love. How does a mother forgive the man who harmed her child? Love. This depth of love cannot be self-generated. It can only come from God's supernatural power.

God loves us no matter what. In the same manner, he tells us to love others with his love and so reflect his love in the world. Two thousand years ago, contemporary observers of the early church were amazed by the way Christians conducted themselves, saying "See how very much they love one another." We can love like that today as we ask God to let his love flow through us to others.

*"In order to love our neighbor
we must see that God
is the cause of love. . . .
You cannot love your neighbor
unless you love God.
God must be loved first
in order that we may love
our neighbor in God."*

BERNARD OF CLAIRVAUX

GOD'S WORD

MARK 12:30–31 "'Love the Lord your God with all your heart and with all your soul and with all your mind and with all your strength.' The second is this: 'Love your neighbor as yourself.' There is no commandment greater than these."

MATTHEW 5:43–44 "You have heard that it was said, 'Love your neighbor and hate your enemy.' But I tell you, love your enemies and pray for those who persecute you."

1 CORINTHIANS 13:4–7, 13 Love is patient, love is kind. It does not envy, it does not boast, it is not proud. It does not dishonor others, it is not self-seeking, it is not easily angered, it keeps no record of wrongs. Love does not delight in evil but rejoices with the truth. It always protects, always trusts, always hopes, always perseveres. . . . And now these three remain: faith, hope and love. But the greatest of these is love.

1 PETER 4:8 Above all, love each other deeply, because love covers over a multitude of sins.

1 JOHN 4:7, 19 Dear friends, let us love one another, for love comes from God. Everyone who loves has been born of God and knows God. . . . We love because he first loved us.

JOHN 15:13 (NLT) "There is no greater love than to lay down one's life for one's friends."

JOB APPLICATION

1. How does understanding God's love for us help us to love others, especially the unlovable?

2. What are the benefits of asking God to give us his love for people, especially those hard to love?

3. Name some practical ways you can demonstrate your love for Jesus?

GOD'S JOB: HONOR
OUR JOB: HONOR

It is human nature to want attention, recognition or the praise of men. Many of us strive to win some distinction that sets us apart from the rest. While it is admirable to always pursue excellence, it is disgraceful to seek glory for one's self. God says, "He who honors me, I will honor." The way to become a truly honorable person is not by seeking honor, but seeking to honor God. The person who loses awareness of himself in the midst of honoring and serving God is the same one God puts in a spotlight as a true role model.

But we must not honor God to get honor. We honor God because he alone is worthy of honor. The moment we catch ourselves pursuing self-honor, even in doing honorable things, we should immediately stop and recalibrate our motives. In this way, we will not forfeit the opportunity to be honored by God. He knows our hearts, and it is the pure in heart, the person truly oblivious of self, that God delights to honor. It's one of those divine surprises that God loves to bestow on those who sincerely, consistently put him first.

"The sovereign God
wants to be loved
for Himself and honored
for Himself, but that is
only part of what He wants.
The other part is that
He wants us to know
that when we have Him
we have everything—
we have all the rest."

A. W. TOZER

GOD'S WORD

1 SAMUEL 2:30 (NLT) "But I will honor those who honor me, and I will despise those who think lightly of me."

1 CHRONICLES 29:12 Wealth and honor come from you; you are the ruler of all things. In your hands are strength and power to exalt and give strength to all.

PSALM 84:11 For the LORD God is a sun and shield; the LORD bestows favor and honor; no good thing does he withhold from those whose walk is blameless.

PROVERBS 3:35 (NLT) The wise inherit honor, but fools are put to shame!

PROVERBS 18:12 Before a downfall the heart is haughty, but humility comes before honor.

LUKE 14:8 "When someone invites you to a wedding feast, do not take the place of honor, for a person more distinguished than you may have been invited."

JOHN 12:26 "Whoever serves me must follow me; and where I am, my servant also will be. My Father will honor the one who serves me."

PROVERBS 14:31 Whoever oppresses the poor shows contempt for their Maker, but whoever is kind to the needy honors God.

JOB APPLICATION

1. In what instances are you tempted to seek honor for yourself?

2. What advantage is there in seeking God's honor over your own?

3. How will your life change if you don't care about the praise of men?

GOD'S JOB: DEFEAT EVIL
OUR JOB: RESIST EVIL

Evil exists. To deny that is to deny reality. The Bible says that all evil finds its genesis in one being, a fallen angel named Lucifer or Satan. God made Lucifer one of the most beautiful and powerful of all angels. However, Lucifer used his free will long ago to rebel against God and led one-third of heaven's angels against their Creator. As a consequence, God expelled them from heaven. Today, Satan is literally hell bent on leading all of mankind into a downward spiral away from God.

Satan is not God's equal, nor is he equal to Jesus, God's Son. Satan is not God's dark counterpart. He is a created being on the level of Michael the archangel. The Scriptures make it clear that Satan's days are numbered, and that God will defeat Satan and all evil one day. In the meantime, evil continues to wreak havoc on us all. This spiritual warfare is uglier than any horror or science fiction movie you've ever seen.

Fortunately, you and I don't have to worry about defeating Satan or his demonic forces. We couldn't even if we wanted to. Our job is to resist evil—to say no when tempted, to call wrong what it is. We need to depend on God's Holy Spirit for the power to escape or withstand the assaults of wicked people, as well as invisible enemies. What a comfort to know that God will step in, fight, and win on our behalf. In the end, his triumph over evil will also be our victory.

"Put very simply, Satan's power in the world is everywhere. Yet wherever men and women walk in the Spirit, sensitive to the anointing they have from God, that power of his just evaporates. There is a line drawn by God, a boundary where by virtue of his own very presence Satan's writ does not run. Let God but occupy all the space himself, and what room is left for the evil one?"

WATCHMAN NEE

GOD'S WORD

JAMES 4:7 Submit yourselves, then, to God. Resist the devil, and he will flee from you.

1 JOHN 4:4 You, dear children, are from God and have overcome them, because the one who is in you is greater than the one who is in the world.

2 THESSALONIANS 3:3 But the Lord is faithful, and he will strengthen you and protect you from the evil one.

JOHN 10:29 "My Father, who has given them to me, is greater than all; no one can snatch them out of my Father's hand."

EPHESIANS 6:13 Therefore put on the full armor of God, so that when the day of evil comes, you may be able to stand your ground, and after you have done everything, to stand.

ROMANS 12:21 Do not be overcome by evil, but overcome evil with good.

REVELATION 20:1–2, 10 And I saw an angel coming down out of heaven, having the key to the Abyss and holding in his hand a great chain. He seized the dragon, that ancient serpent, who is the devil, or Satan. . . . And the devil . . . was thrown into the lake of burning sulfur, where the beast and the false prophet had been thrown. They will be tormented day and night for ever and ever.

JOB APPLICATION

1. Why do some people deny the existence of Satan and/or evil?

2. What do you have to do to survive attacks from the devil?

3. What are the pieces of the armor of God (see Ephesians 6:10–20)?

GOD'S JOB: RESURRECT
OUR JOB: WORSHIP

Death is ugly. If you've ever gazed upon a dead person, you can't help but feel a deep sense of dark finality. While death comes to each of us, it is not the end of the story. God made people to be immortal, meaning that they will live on after their bodies die and decompose. The Scriptures tell us that all humans will be raised from the dead with a new body to face the judgment throne of God. Those who know, love and follow Jesus Christ will enter heaven to enjoy God and his kingdom forever. Those who reject Jesus will be banished from God.

How unspeakable it will be to finally stand before the splendor and beauty of God the Father, God the Son, and God the Holy Spirit—one God in three persons. Everyone will be awestruck, and shout in total unison that Jesus Christ is Lord. But how tragic it will be for unbelievers to finally taste the wonder and beauty of his glory, only to be cast from paradise forever! Yet, the true believer will worship God for his infinite grace, mercy and love. Death is coming. So is our resurrection. By trusting Christ, you can worship him now in Spirit and in truth, and one day in person forever and ever. We are one day closer to that great day. So get ready, and start practicing your worship right now.

"You don't have a soul.
You are a soul.
You have a body."

C. S. LEWIS

GOD'S WORD

1 THESSALONIANS 4:13–17   Brothers and sisters, we do not want you to be uninformed about those who sleep in death, so that you do not grieve like the rest of mankind, who have no hope. For we believe that Jesus died and rose again, and so we believe that God will bring with Jesus those who have fallen asleep in him. According to the Lord's word, we tell you that we who are still alive, who are left until the coming of the Lord, will certainly not precede those who have fallen asleep. For the Lord himself will come down from heaven, with a loud command, with the voice of the archangel and with the trumpet call of God, and the dead in Christ will rise first. After that, we who are still alive and are left will be caught up together with them in the clouds to meet the Lord in the air. And so we will be with the Lord forever.

1 CORINTHIANS 15:51-52   Listen, I tell you a mystery: We will not all sleep, but we will all be changed – in a flash, in the twinkling of an eye, at the last trumpet. For the trumpet will sound, the dead will be raised imperishable, and we will be changed.

PHILIPPIANS 3:20–21 (NLT)   But we are citizens of heaven, where the Lord Jesus Christ lives. And we are eagerly waiting for him to return as our Savior. He will take our weak mortal bodies and change them into glorious bodies like his own, using the same power with which he will bring everything under his control.

REVELATION 4:11   "You are worthy, our Lord and God, to receive glory and honor and power, for you created all things, and by your will they were created and have their being."

JOB APPLICATION

1. Since earth is not our permanent residence, how should we then live?

2. How should we view death in light of the resurrection?

3. What can you do now to prepare for worshiping God face-to-face?

GOD'S JOB: JUDGE
OUR JOB: AGREE

As unpleasant as it sounds, there will be a final judgment, in which every human since the beginning of time will appear before God Almighty to determine his or her eternal destiny. This will be the dramatic conclusion of the age of man. It will also be the breathtaking start to the endless reign of the King of Kings. No one will be exempt from judgment; no one can escape. We will all stand before the Judge, and, one by one, he will separate his true followers from the rest. The bad news is that the non-believers, God-haters and religious pretenders will be cast out from God's presence. As C. S. Lewis observed, if people weren't interested in being in a relationship with God during their brief years on earth, why would they possibly want to spend all eternity with him?

For God's people, those who genuinely put faith in Jesus as Savior and Lord, there is good news. Evil will be defeated, Satan will be doomed forever, and death will be put to death once and for all. One thing will unite the winners and losers—all will agree that God's judgment is right, fair and just. There will be no objections, no appeals. This is the ultimate Supreme Court, and God's verdict will be decisive and irrevocable. Believers will begin their endless days in paradise; the rest will be destined to a very real hell.

Some don't want to believe in judgment, heaven or hell. There is only one way to find out. This is the great cosmic gamble, and what we believe now really does matter later. Trust Christ and live, or reject him and suffer forever. Today is the day of salvation. Say "yes" to Jesus while you can. Why take a chance by refusing his gracious offer of eternal life?

"He who loveth God
with all his heart feareth
not death, nor punishment,
nor judgment, nor hell,
because perfect love giveth
sure access to God. But he
who still delighteth in sin,
no marvel if he is afraid
of death and judgment."

THOMAS À KEMPIS

GOD'S WORD

HEBREWS 9:27 People are destined to die once, and after that to face judgment.

2 CORINTHIANS 5:10 For we must all appear before the judgment seat of Christ, so that each of us may receive what is due us for the things done while in the body, whether good or bad.

REVELATION 20:12–15 And I saw the dead, great and small, standing before the throne, and books were opened. Another book was opened, which is the book of life. The dead were judged according to what they had done as recorded in the books. The sea gave up the dead that were in it, and death and Hades gave up the dead that were in them, and each person was judged according to what they had done. Then death and Hades were thrown into the lake of fire. The lake of fire is the second death. Anyone whose name was not found written in the book of life was thrown into the lake of fire.

MATTHEW 12:36–37 "But I tell you that everyone will have to give account on the day of judgment for every empty word they have spoken. For by your words you will be acquitted, and by your words you will be condemned."

ROMANS 8:1 There is now no condemnation for those who are in Christ Jesus.

ROMANS 2:5–6 But because of your stubbornness and your unrepentant heart, you are storing up wrath against yourself for the day of God's wrath, when his righteous judgment will be revealed. God "will repay each person according to what they have done."

GENESIS 18:25 "Far be it from you to do such a thing—to kill the righteous with the wicked, treating the righteous and the wicked alike. Far be it from you! Will not the Judge of all the earth do right?"

JOB APPLICATION

1. Why is it necessary for God to judge evil and ungodliness?

2. What can prevent you from incurring the condemning wrath of God?

3. Why is God the only one worthy to rightly judge mankind?

GOD'S JOB: RESTORE
OUR JOB: REJOICE

There was a time when all creation was perfect. Then man sinned, introducing physical decay, separation from God and ultimately death. Sin threw everything into a state of chaos. Animals preyed on other animals. Natural disasters like floods, tornadoes, hurricanes, earthquakes, tsunamis, wildfires and droughts wreaked unspeakable destruction. Man's relationships with others spiraled out of control, bringing conflict, hate and disunity. Sin made a colossal mess of everything. The apostle Paul tells us that the whole creation is groaning in frustration, waiting to be liberated from its bondage to decay. Even creation knows that things are not as they were intended to be, and it looks forward to the return to its original state of perfection.

Thankfully, God will restore all things one day. He will make right all that is wrong. Jesus says, "Behold, I am making all things new." His job is to lift the curse and restore his creation and, more importantly, us. He will return his creatures to that pure, holy, rapturous condition that Adam and Eve once enjoyed long ago. One day we who have received Jesus Christ as Savior and Lord will be like him. Knowing this, we can fulfill our job by rejoicing in this glorious hope and precious promise now, on that day when our faith becomes sight, and forever more.

"All their life in this world . . .
had only been the cover
and the title page; now at last
they were beginning
Chapter One of the Great Story
which no one on earth has read,
which goes on forever,
in which every chapter
is better than the one before."

C. S. LEWIS

GOD'S WORD

1 CORINTHIANS 2:9–10 (NLT)   That is what the Scriptures mean when they say, "No eye has seen, no ear has heard, and no mind has imagined what God has prepared for those who love him."

REVELATION 21:1 (ESV)   Then I saw a new heaven and a new earth, for the first heaven and the first earth had passed away.

ISAIAH 33:17   Your eyes will see the king in his beauty and view a land that stretches afar.

REVELATION 21:5 (ESV)   And he who was seated on the throne said, "Behold, I am making all things new."

JOHN 14:1–3 (ESV)   "Let not your hearts be troubled. Believe in God; believe also in me. In my Father's house are many rooms. If it were not so, would I have told you that I go to prepare a place for you? And if I go and prepare a place for you, I will come again and will take you to myself, that where I am you may be also."

ROMANS 8:22–23   We know that the whole creation has been groaning as in the pains of childbirth right up to the present time. Not only so, but we ourselves, who have the firstfruits of the Spirit, groan inwardly as we wait eagerly for our adoption to sonship, the redemption of our bodies.

1 CORINTHIANS 15:53–55 (NLT)   For our dying bodies must be transformed into bodies that will never die; our mortal bodies must be transformed into immortal bodies. Then, when our dying bodies have been transformed into bodies that will never die, this Scripture will be fulfilled: "Death is swallowed up in victory. O death, where is your victory? O death, where is your sting?"

REVELATION 21:4   "'He will wipe every tear from their eyes. There will be no more death' or mourning or crying or pain, for the old order of things has passed away."

JOB APPLICATION

1. What excites you most about the restoration of God's creation?

2. How can the hope of no suffering, crying or death impact you today?

3. What emotions do you think will describe the experience of a perfect world that never ends?

AFTERWORD

Through the preceding pages, we have contrasted what the Scriptures says about God's job and ours as it applies to everyday life. But just knowing the differences isn't really enough. Biblical faith involves acting on knowledge and truth. For example, you may believe that a 777 jet may be capable of transporting you safely from here to Tokyo, but you don't really exercise faith until you step on that plane and take off.

And so it is with God, and more specifically with his Son, Jesus. John 1:12 promises, "Yet to all who did receive him [Jesus], to those who believed in his name, he [God] gave the right to become children of God." To receive Jesus and believe in his name is not just believing his claims to be the Son of God and the only way to know God personally (John 14:6). It is to acknowledge that you are a sinner in need of the forgiveness only he can provide through the cross, agree to turn from a life of independence to a life of dependence on Christ, and to personally accept his gift of salvation as your own.

In other words, you can't appreciate the gospel—which means "Good News"—until you comprehend the bad news, namely that you are eternally separated from God by your sin. We all miss the mark of God's standard. You and I are incapable of earning, in our own power, God's favor. But the Bible tells us that Jesus came to save the lost, to die so that we might live forever, to rise again so that we might rise as well to live with him forever.

If you have never taken Jesus up on his gracious offer of eternal life, now is a great time to do it. We receive Christ through prayer as an act of our will. The following is a suggested prayer:

> *Lord Jesus, I need you. I realize that I have been self-centered. I have done and thought things I should not have, and I have not done and thought the things I should have. I realize that I cannot reach moral perfection without you. Thank you for paying the penalty for my sins when you died on the cross so that I could live forever with you. I receive the salvation you offer as a loving gift from a merciful God. Come into my life and make me the kind of person you want me to be. Amen.*

If receiving Christ is the desire of your heart and you prayed this prayer, you can be assured right now that you have crossed over from eternal separation from God into eternal life with him (1 John 5:13). And Jesus promises that he will never leave you or forsake you (Hebrews 13:5). Your salvation is secure from this day forward (John 10:28–30).

And to all who have read this book, regardless of where you are in your journey of faith, it is my prayer that you will go forward with greater clarity and resolve to do your *job* to the best of our ability, all because God has done and is doing *his job* with amazing love and faithfulness.

If you do this, I have no doubt that the best is yet to come for your life.

ACKNOWLEDGMENTS

The writer of Hebrews speaks of us being "surrounded by such a great cloud of witnesses" (Hebrews 12:1), a heavenly throng of great, wise and godly saints who are cheering us on in our journey. I believe there are also a great cloud of witnesses on earth cheering us on—people who encourage us when we want to give up or provide us with constructive criticisms that hone us as "iron sharpens iron" (Proverbs 27:17).

I can't possibly name all of the kind people who cheered and guided me in the writing of this book, but I do want to say thank you to some who stand out. First, to my wife, Diana Schick, an accomplished writer of more than twenty-four Bible study books, a special word of thanks for providing honest feedback and strong edits to make the book more readable and practical. Then to my longtime friend, Ellen Santilli Vaughn, who was the very first person with whom I shared my idea of this book and who graciously challenged me to go for it. Ellen's candid and seasoned perspectives as a *New York Times* bestselling author helped me view this project with very realistic expectations. And lastly, I want to express my appreciation to everyone who endorsed this work early on, people for whom I have the highest respect for their keen intellect, extraordinary love and genuine Christlikeness—Ellen Vaughn, Marabel Morgan, Joanne Kemp, Frank Turek, Steven V. Taylor, Art Lindsley, David Bock, David Aikman and Jerry Leachman. What an honor to have such wonderful people add their blessings to this project.

RECOMMENDED READING

Basic Christianity, John R. W. Stott

Born Again, Chuck Colson

Can Man Live Without God?, Ravi Zacharias

Celebration of Discipline, Richard J. Foster

The Confessions (of St. Augustine)

The Cost of Discipleship, Dietrich Bonhoeffer

Evidence That Demands a Verdict, Josh McDowell

The God Who Is There, Francis A. Schaeffer

Humility, Andrew Murray

I Don't Have Enough Faith to Be an Atheist, Norman Geisler and Frank Turek

I'm Glad You Asked, Ken Boa and Larry Moody

The Imitation of Christ, Thomas à Kempis

The Kneeling Christian, (Anonymous)

Know Why You Believe, Paul E. Little

Knowing God, J. I. Packer

Knowledge of the Holy, A. W. Tozer

Mere Christianity, C. S. Lewis

My Utmost for His Highest, Oswald Chambers

Pilgrim's Progress, John Bunyan

The Practice of the Presence of God, Brother Lawrence

Psalm 23: The Song of a Passionate Heart, David Roper

The Purpose Driven Life, Rick Warren

The Pursuit of God, A. W. Tozer

Screwtape Letters, C. S. Lewis

What Is the Father Like?, W. Phillip Keller

Who Is This Jesus?, Michael Greene

Who Made God?, Ravi Zacharias and Norman Geisler

With Christ in the School of Prayer, Andrew Murray

ABOUT THE AUTHOR

Michael Wm. Schick is a strategic communications consultant in Washington, DC. He has served as a television director/producer, as a press spokesman for a US Senator, and in leadership positions at major companies and nonprofit organizations. Michael is an honors graduate of the University of South Carolina, a former fellow at the C. S. Lewis Institute and the editor of twenty-three books. Michael and his wife, Diana, have two daughters and reside in Reston, Virginia.